Fairy Tale Time

Fairy Tale Time

Illustrated by
Nikolai Ustinov

HODDER AND STOUGHTON
LONDON SYDNEY AUCKLAND TORONTO

Contents

British Library Cataloguing in Publication Data

Ustinov, N.
   Fairy tale time.
   I. Title
   823′.914[3]   PZ8
    ISBN 0-340-39233-9

Copyright © Verlag J. F. Schreiber, Esslingen 1985
English translation copyright © Hodder and Stoughton Ltd 1987

First published 1985
First published in Great Britain 1987

English text by Samantha Norman

Published by Hodder and Stoughton Children's Books,
a division of Hodder and Stoughton Ltd,
Mill Road, Dunton Green, Sevenoaks, Kent TN13 2YJ

Photoset by Tunbridge Wells Typesetting Services Ltd,
Tunbridge Wells, Kent

Printed in Spain

The Rain Maiden

It is not widely known but the sun has two helpers. One is the gentle Rain Maiden, who draws the clouds across the sky when the sun gets too hot and squeezes raindrops from them to refresh and revive all living things. But the other is the dreaded Flame Man, who tears up the Rain Maiden's clouds and banishes them from the sky. Their bitter feud amuses the kind old sun, but they are sworn enemies none the less, for they are as different from one another as fire from water. The Flame Man is fierce and quick as lightning, while the tender Rain Maiden is slow and sleepy. Indeed, the soft pitter-patter of steady rainfall is quite enough to send her into a deep sleep.

And that is exactly what happened a hundred years ago when, one summer morning, the Rain Maiden just curled up lazily on a soft pillowy white cloud and fell fast asleep. Left to the merciless Flame Man, the sky

became hotter and hotter, and although the earth creaked and groaned and begged for water, still the Rain Maiden did not stir.

This drought became terribly serious for the people of the tiny farming village which nestled snugly in the foothills of a vast mountain range. Their crops were beginning to wither and die and their cattle were so tired and thirsty without the nourishing mountain springs that they were too weak even to bother swishing their tails at the gloating swarms of flies.

Only one person was enjoying the

drought, and that was the valley meadow farmer who owned the lush green water meadows by the river. His crops still had enough moisture to withstand the heat. And one morning, as he stood proudly admiring his land, Old Mother Stine, his kindly neighbour, came trundling over the hill towards him, heavily laden with a huge wooden tub.

"Could you spare me a little water for my sheep, meadow farmer," she asked.

"Certainly I will," the farmer replied, "but I will beg a favour of you in return."

"What is that?" asked Old Mother Stine.

"Well, your son Andrees has asked for my daughter Dörte's hand in marriage."

"How lovely," said the old lady, who already knew that the couple wanted to wed.

"You don't understand," said the farmer, growing red in the face with anger. "No daughter of mine will ever marry a poor farm lad, even if she does love him. The marriage must not take place."

Mother Stine calmly replied: "If I may say so, you are being rather silly. We won't always be poor, and when the rain comes again, the river will

flood your meadows and drown your crops and you won't be rich any more."

"Well that's hardly likely," snorted the meadow farmer irritably, "I doubt

if the Rain Maiden will ever wake up again".

"Then I shall just have to make her wake up," the old woman replied heartily.

"And pigs will fly," retorted the farmer unkindly. "Nobody has the power to do that."

Old Mother Stine grinned. "Well, as a matter of fact, I have. My grandmother did it once, and she told me the rhyme which has the power to wake the Rain Maiden."

What she did not tell him, however, was that she had, by now, forgotten the rhyme and that she would need Dörte to help her, because only a young girl could approach the Rain Maiden.

"What a ridiculous fairy tale!" chortled the farmer. "Anyway, I don't care if the Rain Maiden never wakes up; I rather enjoy the hot weather. But if you insist you *can* wake her, I'll wager my daughter's hand in marriage that you can't."

"Done," said the old lady and, when they'd shaken hands to seal the bet, Dörte, who had been eaves-dropping on their conversation, came running out of the farmhouse to help her old neighbour carry the water-filled tub over the hill to where Andrees was waiting with the thirsty sheep. Just as they set the tub down, they heard a loud and piercing voice

ring out through the valley.

"Quick, quick," it hissed, and again, "quick, quick," and a ferocious little figure came darting like a firefly through the meadow towards them. His long, burning red hair flickered like flames round his scarlet face and his clothes flapped in fire-red tatters around his spindly legs. He ran right through the scattering herd of frightened sheep and with his long, thin fingers stabbed viciously at them and singed their poor coats. As he ran, he sang in a loud raucous voice,

"To steam turn the seas,
And the rivers run dry,
Parched are the trees,
When the Flame Man comes by."

"It's the Flame Man," whispered Old Mother Stine, "he's reciting the rhyme I'd forgotten." But the Flame Man overheard and vanished.

"Oh goodness! Half the rhyme's missing," said the old lady. Dörte and

Andrees sat quietly while she cast her mind back many years to when she was a little girl and her grandmother had taught her the magical chant.

"Eureka!" she shouted suddenly. "The rest of the rhyme goes like this:

Come soon, come soon
You must to wake me,
Or Mother to the underworld
will take me.

Now Dörte, repeat that after me." So

Dörte repeated the rhyme ten times, until she knew it off by heart.

"Well," said Andrees, "What we must do now is find out where the Rain Maiden lives, and I know just the person to ask!"

With that, he set off in search of the Flame Man, who was not hard to find because a vivid trail of scorch marks traced his path through the meadow. When Andrees reached the place where the Flame Man was basking like a lizard in the sun, the

forest and that the only way to get there is through the hollow by a big willow tree." By now, the Flame Man was so angry that he looked as if he might explode, so Andrees thanked him cheekily, and beat a hasty retreat to join the others.

Andrees and Dörte decided to start their adventure the following day. Early next morning, well before the first cockcrow and in pitch darkness, when the Flame Man's power was weakest, the young couple met in the valley meadows and, with only a lantern to guide them, made their way through the eerie forest to its furthermost edge, where the silhouette of a line of ancient willow trees loomed against the dark sky.

Andrees marched up to the tallest tree and began to recite the rhyme. As he finished, the roots of the tree split apart, revealing a tunnel leading down into the ground. The astonished young couple clambered into the gaping hollow, their teeth chattering with the chill of the dank earth, and slipped and slithered their way down the spiralling tunnel.

After many hours of struggling along beneath the earth's surface, a single shaft of sunlight guided them upwards at last into the stifling heat of the morning sun. Andrees and Dörte

little demon called over to him: "Hey, you, I suppose you are looking for the Rain Maiden?"

"Suppose that I was," said Andrees casually. "I certainly wouldn't ask you because you're too stupid."

At this the Flame Man began leaping about like an enraged firecracker.

"Too stupid, am I? Too stupid, eh! Well, we'll see which one of us is so stupid that he doesn't even know that the Rain Maiden lives beyond the

stood blinking like moles in the dazzling light, but when they were finally able to see around them, they found themselves on a tiny path on the other side of the mountains. Some ancient instinct within them recognised this as the kingdom of the Rain Maiden. But even in this sacred land, the drought had left pitiful scars, for the once lush green meadows were parched and dry and the grass crumbled like ashes beneath their feet.

They followed the little path as it wound its way beside the dried bed of a great river, which had once brimmed with the cool clear water of the mountain springs and bubbled with leaping fish. After a long avenue of trees, the craggy path led the weary travellers into a huge park, in the middle of which was a large lake, empty now but for a small pool of stagnant, muddy water where a strange water bird stood sleeping on one leg. Behind this pitiful sight, the fierce sun shone down on to the Rain Maiden's stone palace.

"You must go alone from here," said Andrees, and he sank down,

exhausted, to his knees and watched Dörte walk to the edge of the lake. All of a sudden she leapt back in surprise, for there on the ground in front of her lay a beautiful lady, her face so pale and peaceful that Dörte was not sure if she was alive or dead. This must surely be the Rain Maiden, she thought. Dörte dropped to her knees, put her mouth close to the Rain Maiden's ear and repeated the rhyme.

No sooner had she finished than a terrific bolt of lightning struck the treetops and a deafening shriek rent the air. For a split second, the outline of the Flame Man's hideous form emblazoned itself on the stone walls of the palace, and then vanished.

"Oh, Rain Maiden," pleaded Dörte tearfully, "wake up. Do please wake up, you have slept for far too long."

The Rain Maiden half-opened her large, sleepy, blue eyes. "Does my beautiful water bird still soar over the lake?" she asked.

"No, Rain Maiden, he stands in the mud and sleeps."

"Then does my sparkling river still run through the land?"

"No, no, Rain Maiden, it is all dried up."

"Shame on me!" cried the Rain

Maiden. "It is time I did something." Turning to Dörte, she said, "If you would fill that jug with what little water there is left, we shall make rain together."

When Dörte had managed to fill the jug from the last trickles of a nearby spring, the Rain Maiden asked her to fetch the key to her castle. "To do that, you will have to cross the stream, but whatever happens, do not fear, nothing will harm you."

Dörte began to make her way to the castle where the key hung on a rusty nail and glinted in the sun. But as she waded into the squelching mud of the stream bed, a flame-red hand darted out of it and snatched at her ankles. Dörte screamed and leapt into the air, and was all for going back, but the Rain Maiden's calm voice told her to keep going and so, with her heart in her mouth, she went on bravely and to her relief soon reached the key. She thrust out her hand to grab it but, as she did so, the Flame Man's hand shot out of the stone wall and a sheet of fire zig-zagged over the key, turning it white with heat, so that Dörte dared not touch it. She looked around her help-lessly and then, quick as a flash, she remembered the water in the jug and she threw it over the demon's hand. The Flame Man let out a blood-curdling scream and vanished.

Dörte shivered but, without wasting any more time, took the key and unlocked the enormous door to the castle. As the voice told her, she went to the large well in the entrance hall and, pushing with all her might, lifted the lid. Strange watery vapours rose from the murky depths, and as they mingled with the air, a fine mist formed, a clammy fog gathered, and soon thick black rain clouds were swirling around her face.

"Now clap your hands," ordered the Rain Maiden, who had suddenly appeared beside her. Dörte did so and obediently the clouds filed past her, on and on, upwards into the sky. Before she knew it, it was pouring with rain.

The Rain Maiden thanked Dörte most gratefully and told her that if she had not come in time her mother would have banished her to the underworld. Before they parted for ever, the Rain Maiden pressed a turquoise ring into Dörte's hand. "A keepsake," she said and vanished into the castle.

When Dörte returned she found Andrees lying flat on his back, enjoying the splish-splash of the

refreshing rain on his face. Together they set off for home in a little boat which the Rain Maiden had sent especially for them. The boat seemed to know exactly where it was going and bobbed gently along the twisting, turning course of the swelling river, until it glided smoothly to the bank where the meadow farmer and Old Mother Stine were waiting for them.

"Look what the Rain Maiden gave me, Father," said Dörte, proudly displaying the lovely ring. A wry smile crept over the old man's face.

"Andrees will have to buy you another one now." And turning to Old Mother Stine he said: "I think you've more than won your bet."

Needless to say, they all lived very happily ever after, but from that day on, the Rain Maiden never fell asleep again.

The Wild Man of the Forest

Once upon a time, there was a young prince who had heard of a princess in the neighbouring kingdom who was so beautiful and innocent that when she drank red wine, a pink blush glowed at her throat. The prince was enchanted by the many stories he had heard of her and decided that he would like to marry her, so one day he waved goodbye to the king and queen and rode off alone to find her.

On the way to the castle where the princess lived, he had to go through a dark and dangerous forest where he was ambushed by a band of hungry robbers. These wicked men kicked and beat him, stole his horse and fine robes and left him for dead. The prince did not die, but his wounds took such a long time to heal that he was forced to stay in the forest and learn to feed himself from the wild berries and beechnuts, and drink water from the clear forest springs.

The months passed and the prince's hair and beard grew long and unruly, and the few clothes which the thieves had left him were in tatters. Indeed, he began to look more like a wild creature than a noble prince.

Then, one fateful day, the father of the beautiful princess came hunting in the forest, with many huntsmen and servants, and he caught sight of a

wild-looking man hiding in the undergrowth. He ordered his huntsmen to capture the creature, and after a long and desperate struggle, the king's men overcame the wild man and bound and gagged him and, tying him across a horse's back, led him all the way to the king's palace.

Once more the prince was badly injured, only this time his jaw was so bruised from the brutal blows the huntsmen had dealt him that he was unable to speak and tell them who he really was. And he was unable to protest when the king ordered his men to throw him into an empty bear-cage with thick iron bars. As the

door slammed against his freedom he heard the king hand over the key to the queen with strict instructions never to let the prisoner out, for he was wild and dangerous and would murder them all in their beds.

As the days passed, the king grew very proud of his rare catch and invited all his friends to the palace to see the wild man of the forest, and they would taunt and tease him as if he were a poor dumb animal caged in a zoo.

During the long and tormented days of his captivity, the wild man would amuse himself by watching the princess playing by his cage. Some-times she would peer through the

bars curiously at him, but when she noticed that his eyes were sad and sorrowful she would look away again. She had no idea that she was the cause of his misery.

On the days when the princess did not come to play by his cage, the wild man would pass the time watching the spider in the corner of his cage spinning its web, and admiring the bees who flew into his cage from the nearby beehive, busily collecting the princess's favourite honey. One day, the prince noticed that one of the bees had become tangled in the spider's web and was desperately struggling to free itself.

"Poor little fellow," said the prince, "I know just what it's like to be a prisoner. I'll set you free." So, very carefully, he untangled the bee from the sticky web and let it go. Before it flew away, the bee did a very strange thing; it flew three times round the wild man's head, as if it was trying to thank him for his kindness.

The weary and unhappy hours became days, the days became weeks and the weeks became months, and the prince began to give up hope of ever escaping. Then, one day, while the king was out hunting, and the queen was taking her afternoon rest, the princess came to play by the wild man's cage. He watched her throwing and catching an exquisite little ball made of the finest golden threads, which was her very favourite toy. All of a sudden, the princess became careless and threw the ball too high, and she gasped in horror as she

watched it soar through the air, through the bars of the wild creature's cage, and land in his lap.

"Please give me back my ball," she shouted. But the wild man of the

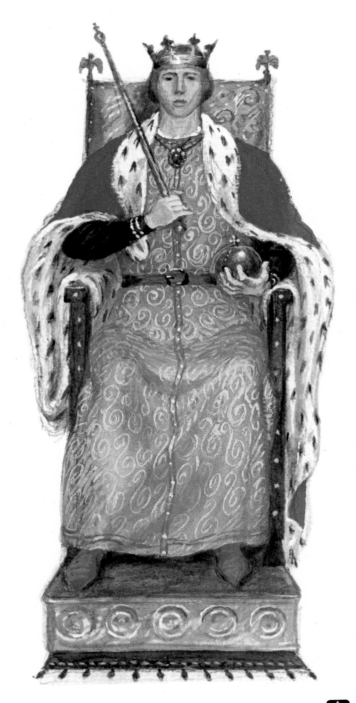

forest shook his shaggy head and refused to return the ball. Then the princess began to cry and the wild man softened.

"I'll make a bargain with you," he said. "I'll give you back your ball if you open my cage."

"I can't," wailed the princess. "Mama has the key and Papa would be furious if I were to let you out."

"In that case," replied the wild man, "you won't get your ball back."

"If I told my father," said the princess crossly, "he'd make you give it back." The wild man chuckled at the expression of fury on her face.

"Then tell him," he said, "but if you do, I'll tear it into a thousand pieces."

At that, the princess turned and

ran off to her mother's bed-chamber and when she peeped her head round the door and saw that she was still asleep, she crept in, slid her hand under the pillow where her mother always kept the key to the cage, and ran back with it to the wild man. Then she handed him the key and he gave her back her ball and ran off to freedom. The princess was scared when she saw the strange creature leaping through the palace and she ran to her mother, who was awake by now, and, realising that the key was missing, had alerted the guards. Huntsmen, guards and soldiers were called to find the escaped prisoner, but the wild man had disappeared.

The joyful prince arrived home at last, and once he had shaved off his

news that the wild man had escaped. The king vowed before all his courtiers, "I shall search the length and breadth of the forest until I find him again," and with that he rode off. This time, the prince was waiting for him and he watched the huntsmen leave the king to look for the wild man. When they were out of sight, he sprang, and knocked the king from his horse. Then the prince tied him up and took him back to his own castle, and threw the king into the cell he had prepared for him and treated him as the king had himself treated the wild man.

Many weeks later, when the king's beard and hair had grown long, and his clothes were in tatters, the prince came to the cell.

"How are you today, wild creature?" he asked.

"Don't mock me," replied the king. "Just tell me what it is you want from me and let me go."

"I shall certainly let you go," said the prince, "on one condition. You once kept the wild man of the forest prisoner and you were cruel to him, but your daughter set him free. I will let you go only if you agree to give your daughter's hand in marriage to that same man."

The king had no way of knowing

beard and cut his hair, his parents recognised him and organised a huge feast to celebrate his return.

Meanwhile, the princess's father had returned from his hunting to the

that this was the man he had known as the wild man of the forest, for the prince was now splendidly handsome and noble in his royal finery. So, although he pretended to agree to the prince's demands, in his heart he refused to allow his precious daughter to be married to such a creature as the wild man, and he sent a secret letter to the queen telling her what had happened and asking her to dress up a lady-in-waiting as though she were the princess and send her to the prince's palace.

The queen did as she was asked, and very soon the lady-in-waiting arrived dressed exactly like the princess. But when she sat down to supper with the prince, she drank some red wine which the prince had ordered specially for her. After the first sip, her throat did not blush pink and the prince knew he had been deceived, and sent her back.

Now the poor old king was at his wits' end. Like it or no, he had to send for the princess herself or he would remain a captive for ever. This he did, and the princess reluctantly set off on the tearful journey to the prince's palace, accompanied by her mother, and all her ladies-in-waiting. On the way, a little bee flew into the carriage and buzzed around the princess's face.

The queen started to flap at it and ordered her servant to kill it, but the princess protested.

"Leave it, Mama, I only wish it would sting me and disfigure my face, then perhaps the wild man would not want me." So the bee was spared its life and flew out of the carriage, and it hovered above them until they reached the castle.

As the prince greeted the princess, he noticed that she had grown even more beautiful than ever, and he was doubly enchanted with her. Something in his heart cried out for him to confess to the princess that he was the wild man and that she had nothing to fear, but he resisted the temptation and kept quiet.

"I would like to see my father," the princess told him.

"You may do so, but only when I have your word of honour that you will marry the wild man," replied the prince. With great reluctance, the princess gave her promise.

The queen was horrified that such a fate should befall her daughter, particularly now she had seen the love which welled in the prince's eyes when he looked at her daughter, so, as the princess gave the prince her promise, she spoke firmly.

"Before I give my daughter's hand in marriage to such a vile creature, he must first pass a test. If he can recognise my daughter from amongst twelve similarly dressed and heavily veiled ladies-in-waiting, then he may have her. If, however, he fails to do this, I demand that my family and I go free from here."

The prince agreed to the test. After all, he thought, it should be easy to recognise the princess by her gracefulness. But, when he had disguised himself as the wild man of the forest and walked in to the hall where the queen was waiting with the twelve veiled ladies, he realised it was not going to be as easy as he thought. He stood facing the long line of identical ladies and scratched his beard thoughtfully.

"Now, you low and despicable

creature," said the queen, "find your princess if you can."

The wild man looked terribly confused. Perhaps, he thought, if I told them a funny story, I could find the princess because she would be the only one who would be too frightened to laugh. But the prince was never very good at telling jokes and, to his dismay, nobody laughed. So the hours passed, and the prince's hopes sank as fast as the rapidly setting sun.

Then, all of a sudden, a little bee flew into the hall and started buzzing round the veiled ladies. After a few minutes, it started to fly in frantic circles around one particular head. Whenever the queen tried to shoo it away, it would just return to the same spot. The delighted prince recognised the little bee as the one he had rescued all those months ago and realised that it was trying to help him. So he strode up to the lady over whom the bee was hovering, pulled her veil aside, and revealed the beautiful face of the princess!

When the princess raised her eyes, and saw the wild man, she burst into tears and sank to her knees and begged for mercy. The prince could bear it no longer. He tore off his wig and beard and, to the princess's

joy, revealed himself as the prince.

That night, the prince's parents threw a huge and lavish feast in honour of their son's engagement. The princess's father had been released by this time, and was overjoyed with the news of his daughter's forthcoming marriage, and because his prison food had been far from delicious, he tucked in heartily to the tremendous banquet.

So, less than a month later, the prince and princess were married and they lived in a state of blissful happiness. Occasionally, when the prince had become king and was busy ruling his kingdom, he would forget to cut his hair or shave, and the princess would say firmly: "Go to the court hairdresser. I don't want to end up married to the wild man of the forest."

Princess Roseblossom

Once upon a time there was a king and queen who had two strapping sons but longed for a daughter. One day the queen gave birth to a little girl who was so beautiful that everyone who saw her fell in love with her.

All the subjects of the kingdom were overjoyed at the news of the

her daughter, he shook his head in sorrow and said: "Your Royal Highness, it is my sad duty to tell you that the princess will bring mortal danger to her brothers."

The queen was overcome with grief and fled to the palace to tell the king the awful news. When she had finished the king became very grave and locked himself away in his chamber. After many days of sombre brooding, he climbed to the ramparts of the castle and announced his decision to the kingdom.

"My loyal subjects! You have, by now, all heard the words of the wise man, and will understand that I have no choice but to banish my daughter from this castle. She will be taken to a strictly guarded tower where no one except myself, the queen, the nursemaid and the nursemaid's daughter will be allowed to see her."

Princess Roseblossom, for that was the child's name, did not seem to mind this lonely life and continued to bring joy to all those who were privileged to see her. Animals loved her too, and her little dog, Quicksilver, who was her only playmate, refused ever to leave her side. However, the princess did have a secret visitor, and a rather mysterious one at that. He was a handsome young king who

royal birth and they celebrated the event as nothing had ever been celebrated before. Only one person stood solemn and alone amongst the jubilant crowds, and this was the wise man. He could see into the future and was treated with fearful respect throughout the land.

When the queen went to him to ask what the future held in store for appeared to her in a vision, dressed in a glorious robe of peacock feathers. Their eyes would meet for a few seconds only, and then he would vanish as suddenly as he had appeared. Roseblossom wept each time he left her but somehow she always knew that he would return, for the princess was deeply in love with the young king.

Then, one sad and fateful day, the king and queen both died of a fever. The whole kingdom was steeped in gloom and all the people grieved because they had been good rulers and were well-loved by their subjects. As soon as the long and miserable period of mourning was over the elder of the two sons, who had been crown prince, turned to his brother and said: "Since I am now the king, it is my decision that we should ignore the gloomy words of the wise old man and free our sister from the tower. She is old enough to be wed now, and I would like to see her happily married. We shall find a husband for her."

And so the two brothers rode off to the tower and released their sister, who was overjoyed to see them.

No sooner had Roseblossom set foot in the outside world, than she began to marvel at the beauty of the kingdom. One day, when she was out walking with her brothers and her faithful little dog, they came upon a large garden. All of a sudden the princess stood stock-still and her mouth fell open in amazement. A peacock was fanning its tail and parading his splendour before her.

Only once before had Roseblossom seen such beauty, and that was in her vision of the handsome young king.

"What do you call that wonderful creature?" she asked her brothers.

"Oh that," they replied, "that's a peacock, they're pretty birds but my goodness, they taste even better than they look."

Princess Roseblossom was horrified: "How could anybody dare to kill

such sacred creatures. From this moment on I swear that I will never marry anyone but the King of the Peacocks and he and I will devote our lives to protecting them."

"You can't be serious, Roseblossom," said the astonished brothers. "There's no such person as the King of the Peacocks."

"Oh yes, there is." Roseblossom was convinced of it now and stood staring wistfully in to the distance as if she could actually see him. Then she turned towards her brothers and begged them: "Oh, please, you must help me to find him."

The princes could not bear to see their sister suffer any more, and so they agreed to help her. They soon began to make plans for their quest. First of all, they decided, Roseblossom's beauty should be made

known far and wide, so they asked the finest artist in the land to paint a picture of her. When this was done, the brothers, who did not really believe that there was such a person as the King of the Peacocks, but were excited by the idea of an adventure, said goodbye to Roseblossom, and set off.

They travelled all over the world and eventually arrived at the end of the earth. The princes were very tired and had begun to lose heart when, to their astonishment, they saw a signpost which said in bold letters: **TO THE CITY OF THE PEACOCK KINGDOM.** The brothers rode off in the direction in which it pointed and found themselves in an amazing city. At every street corner stood a peacock statue; all the houses were painted in the colours of a peacock's plumage and all the townsfolk were dressed in the most dazzling robes of peacock blue.

The princes gazed around them in amazement and kept pinching themselves to make sure they weren't dreaming. And then, all of a sudden, there was a loud fanfare of trumpets and into sight came a golden chariot pulled by twelve of the most magnificent peacocks the brothers had ever seen.

"The king! The king!" the townsfolk cried joyfully, and lo and behold the King of the Peacocks stepped right out in front of them. Of all the sights they had seen that day, surely

this was the most splendid. His long golden hair flowed down his back like a lion's mane and his eyes were as blue as the eyes on a peacock's feather.

Two servants hurried forward and led the dumbstruck princes before the king. With a low bow the brothers explained the purpose of their visit.

"Your Majesty," said the elder brother. "We have come from the ends of the earth to show you a very special picture. It is a portrait of our beautiful sister, Roseblossom, who, in some mysterious way, knows all about you and pleaded with us to come and find you; we hope the picture will explain everything else."

With that they handed the king Roseblossom's portrait. He looked long and hard at the picture and then, to their relief, smiled and said: "If this picture is really a true likeness, then I believe she must be the most beautiful girl in the world."

"It was painted by the finest artist in our kingdom," said the younger brother, "and even he had to admit that it did not do full justice to her beauty."

"May I keep the portrait?" asked the king, rather shyly.

"Only if you promise never to part with it," replied the brothers.

Then the king said: "I shall never part with it as long as you swear on your lives that she is as beautiful as the portrait, and that you will send for her immediately so that I can judge for myself." The brothers promised and were just about to congratulate themselves when the king added: "If you are lying to me, you will both die!"

"Understood," said the brothers and, because they knew that they were telling the truth, calmly allowed themselves to be led away to a well-guarded tower. There they made haste in writing to Roseblossom.

As soon as Roseblossom received the message from her brothers she began to prepare for her journey. She decided to travel by sea and to take only her nursemaid, her nursemaid's daughter and, of course, her trusted companion, Quicksilver. But, just before they left, the wise man made an unexpected visit to the palace, wearing the same solemn expression

he had worn on the day the princess was born.

"Beware the voyage," he said, and vanished. The princess was alarmed, but in her excitement and happiness she soon forgot the warning and made for the ship.

When the small party had been at sea for some days, the princess began to notice a sinister change in her old nursemaid. Once again, Rose-blossom took no notice. Then, one night when the princess was asleep, the nursemaid crept in to the captain's cabin.

"How would you like to be rich?" she hissed. The captain was surprised that she had asked, but replied that he would like it very much.

"Then help me to get rid of the princess," the wicked hag replied, "and when she is gone we will dress my daughter in her fine clothes and present her to the King of the Peacocks as if she was Roseblossom herself. When they are married I shall see to it that you are very well rewarded."

The captain felt sorry for the gentle princess, but he was a greedy man and so he agreed to help the evil nursemaid.

That very night, they crept in to the princess's cabin, picked up the entire bedstead on which she and Quicksilver slept, tossed it into the sea and watched it float away.

The sound of the sea eventually woke Quicksilver, who immediately barked at the princess, and they clung together in terror on the floating bed, waiting to drown.

Then a small miracle happened. From a lighthouse nearby, the keeper noticed a strange shape rocking on the waves and sensed danger. He was

a brave man and immediately set sail in his small boat and brought the half-drowned princess and her little dog to safety.

Once inside the lighthouse keeper's cottage, the princess fell unconscious and lay in a deep sleep for many days. When at last she recovered, she thanked the keeper for looking after her so kindly and asked him to take her to the palace of the King of the Peacocks.

Meanwhile, the treacherous nursemaid and her daughter had arrived in the city, and they stopped off at the nearest inn to put on their finery. The nursemaid was very good at dressing royal princesses, and so everyone believed they were who they said they were.

The king soon heard of their arrival, for the royal princess and her lady in waiting were the talk of the town by this time. But he was a cautious man and decided to go to the inn disguised as a servant so that he could see the princess for himself. When he arrived, however, he was angry to see that the girl's face was so plastered with make-up that it was very hard to tell whether she resembled the portrait or not.

Then the day came when the imposters were invited to a banquet at the palace to meet the king. Still he could not decide whether this girl was as beautiful as her portrait, and he was becoming more and more unhappy. And then it happened! The nursemaid's daughter, who was very spoilt and bad mannered, announced in a loud and piercing voice: "I want some roast peacock! Why isn't it on the menu?"

The king and all the guests were horrified! Eating peacocks was against the law. Now he was in no doubt that the princes had lied to him. He rushed from the table in disgust and raced to the tower in which the two brothers were imprisoned, to reckon with them.

When the princes had heard the awful story they were deeply shocked and asked to be taken to see their sister. At the sight of the brothers the imposters went deathly pale, and while the princes explained that this was not Roseblossom and her lady-in-waiting but the nursemaid and her daughter, the villains crept away and, once outside the palace walls, they fled for their lives and were never seen again.

The king and the princes had hardly noticed their disappearance when the lighthouse keeper entered.

"Your Royal Highness," he said. "Allow me to introduce Princess Roseblossom." As the princess walked gracefully into the crowded hall, all the heads turned. The princes rushed towards her, weeping with delight, to see their sister safe and sound.

The king stood motionless, gazing in turn at the princess and the portrait. Only once before had he seen such beauty; and then the memories of the lovely face which haunted his dreams came flooding back. He sprang forward, swept Roseblossom into his arms and held her tenderly.

At this joyful sight the crowds began cheering and celebrating and Quicksilver turned three somersaults in the air, and the brothers, whose lives were saved, clapped each other on the back.

The lighthouse keeper, who felt that the princess's happiness was reward enough, was given a golden yacht for his part in the adventure, as well as an invitation to the wedding, and Quicksilver was rewarded for his faithfulness to the princess with a basket of biscuits.

And so, except for the nursemaid, her daughter and the captain, they all lived happily ever after. And, although the King of the Peacocks and his queen were never parted, he kept her portrait close by him forever, if only to prove that no painting could capture her true beauty.

The Frog Princess

Once upon a time, in a far away Russian kingdom, there lived a tsar and his three young sons, all of whom were more handsome and brave than any prince in any fairy tale. The tsar's favourite son was Ivan-Tsarevich, the youngest of the three princes.

One day, the tsar assembled his sons before him and said: "My dear children, you are now old enough to find wives for yourselves. Besides, we need a woman's touch around the palace. Go to the palace gates and shoot one arrow each. Wherever your arrows fall, you must go to the owner of that piece of land and ask for his daughter's hand in marriage."

The three princes did as their father commanded, and the eldest son shot an arrow from his bow which landed in a farmer's meadow — right at the feet of his pretty daughter. Then the second son shot his arrow and that landed in the courtyard of a merchant's house just where his lovely daughter was hanging out the washing. And last, but not least, Ivan-Tsarevich fired his arrow, but it soared like a bird through the air and no one saw where it landed. Ivan-Tsarevich set out to look for his arrow and searched until he came to a green pasture where he found a little frog holding the arrow in its mouth.

"Give me back my arrow, little frog," said Ivan-Tsarevich.

"Only if you promise to marry me," croaked the frog.

Ivan-Tsarevich was rather taken aback. "How on earth can I marry a frog?" he asked.

"It is your destiny, Ivan-Tsarevich," answered the frog. So, rather reluctantly, Ivan-Tsarevich picked up the little frog and carried it home.

The marriages were arranged soon afterwards. The eldest prince married the farmer's daughter, the middle son married the merchant's daughter and much to the amusement of everyone else, Ivan-Tsarevich married the frog.

Several days later, the tsar summoned his sons to him and said: "I want each of your wives to bake me a fine loaf of bread for tomorrow's breakfast."

At this, Ivan-Tsarevich hung his head in despair and went home to his little frog.

"Ivan-Tsarevich, why are you sad?" she asked. "Was your father nasty to you?"

"Why shouldn't I be sad?" he answered. "My father commands you to bake a fine loaf of bread for him by tomorrow morning. How can a frog do that?"

But the frog just answered cheerfully, "Don't worry, just go to bed, things always seem brighter in the morning."

Ivan-Tsarevich did as his little frog told him, and while he slept, she shed her frog skin and turned into a beautiful young princess, Vassilissa the Wise. Then she went outside and called out into the night: "Come all my little maids and servants, bake me a loaf of bread as soft as cake, just like the ones I used to eat in my father's palace."

When Ivan-Tsarevich woke the following morning, Vassilissa had changed back into a frog, and presented him with the most beautiful loaf of bread he had ever seen.

The tsar inspected the loaves. Firstly he sent back in disgust the loaf which his eldest son's wife had baked for him, then he shook his head in despair at the loaf his second son presented to him, but when he saw the loaf which the little frog had made for him, his eyes lit up greedily, and he announced for all to hear: "This is the loaf of bread which I shall eat for my breakfast." But, before Ivan-Tsarevich could breathe a sigh of relief, his father gave the three princes another command: "Before the break of day tomorrow, your wives must each weave me a shirt to wear at the great feast tomorrow night." Ivan-Tsarevich went home and hung his head in misery.

"Ivan-Tsarevich," asked the little frog. "Why are you sad? Wasn't your

father pleased with the loaf?"

"Why shouldn't I be sad?" replied Ivan-Tsarevich. "Now my father wants you to weave a shirt for him by tomorrow, but you are only a frog and frogs can't weave."

"Don't despair, go to bed, things always seem brighter in the morning," she replied.

Once again, as Ivan-Tsarevich slept, the little frog changed into Vassilissa the Wise and called to all her maids and servants of the night, "Come weave me a shirt as magnificent as the ones my father used to wear."

No sooner said than done, and when Ivan-Tsarevich awoke in the morning, the little frog was perched on top of the most splendid shirt he had ever seen.

The tsar shook his head at the shirt which his eldest son's wife had made for him and told his second son, "This is more suitable for a stable lad." But when he saw the shirt which the little frog had made, he was overcome with joy and announced proudly: "This is the shirt I shall wear to the feast tonight."

"At last I can be happy," thought Ivan-Tsarevich, but just as he began to smile again, his father said: "Now, my sons, I want you all to bring your wives to the great feast tonight."

Once again, Ivan-Tsarevich hung his head in despair and returned home to his little frog, and when she saw him, she asked: "Why are you sad, Ivan-Tsarevich? Did your father not like the shirt?"

"I have every reason in the world to be sad," replied Ivan-Tsarevich. "My father has asked me to take you to the feast tonight, but how on earth can I face all those people when my wife is a little green frog."

"Don't worry so, Ivan-Tsarevich, you go to the feast alone and I will follow, but when you hear thunder and lightning, don't be afraid, just say to yourself, 'That's my little frog arriving'."

So, Ivan-Tsarevich went to the feast alone, and when his brothers saw him, they laughed and said: "What's wrong, brother? Did you forget your wife, or is she hiding in your pocket?"

At that moment, there was crash of thunder and a bolt of lightning and suddenly a magnificent carriage drew up outside the palace and out of it stepped Vassilissa the Wise, and everyone agreed that she was the most beautiful princess they had ever seen. She floated gracefully through the crowds, took Ivan-Tsarevich by

the hand and led him to the banqueting table, and everyone began to eat and drink and be merry. Vassilissa drank a glass of wine and when she reached the last drop, she poured it carefully into her left sleeve. Then she ate some roast swan and tucked the little bones into her right sleeve. And when she and Ivan-Tsarevich began to dance, she swung

her left arm gracefully in a wide arc and a beautiful lake appeared before the astonished guests. Next, she swung her right arm and the lake was suddenly scattered with magnificent white swans.

The crowds gasped in awe, and whilst everyone marvelled at her

strange magic, Ivan-Tsarevich crept out, and ran back to the palace. When he got there, he found Vassilissa's frog skin and he threw it on to the fire. Then he went to bed and dreamt of the beautiful princess. When Vassilissa returned home and realised what Ivan-Tsarevich had done, she was very sad and tears welled in her lovely eyes.

"What have you done, what have you done?" she cried. "If only you could have waited for me for three more days, I could have been yours for ever, but now you have driven me away and I must leave you." With that, she vanished.

Ivan-Tsarevich was heartbroken and realised he could no longer live without his beautiful princess, and even missed the cheerful little frog. So, that night, he set off to find her.

He travelled far and wide for many years until, one day, he met a very old wise man who stopped him and said, "Greetings, noble prince, where are you going?" When Ivan-Tsarevich had told him his story, the old man gasped. "Oh my goodness, Ivan-Tsarevich, what possessed you to burn that frog skin? You didn't give it to her, so it wasn't yours to take away. You see, Vassilissa the Wise is an enchanted princess and because she was born much cleverer than her father, he was jealous. Out of spite, he put a curse on her and condemned her to live as a frog for three years. I'm afraid I don't know where she is now, but I will give you this ball of yarn and if you follow it wherever it goes, it will eventually lead you to her."

Ivan-Tsarevich thanked the old man with all his heart and went on his way, following the ball of yarn. He went for miles and miles, until he reached a snowy forest, and there amongst the trees Ivan-Tsarevich came face to face with a huge bear. Ivan-Tsarevich grabbed his bow, took aim at the creature and was about to shoot, when the bear said: "Let me live, Ivan-Tsarevich, and one day I will help you." So the young prince allowed the bear to go. Then, suddenly, a drake flew into the air above him. Once more Ivan-Tsarevich took aim and was about to shoot when the drake begged: "Let me live, Ivan-Tsarevich, and one day I will help you." So, Ivan-Tsarevich spared the drake's life, and went on his way. A little while later, a large hare bounded across his path. Once again, Ivan-Tsarevich was about to shoot when the hare turned to him and pleaded: "Let me live, Ivan-Tsarevich, and one day I'll prove useful to you." So, Ivan-Tsarevich spared the hare and went on his way.

Soon the ball of yarn led him out of the forest and down to the deep blue ocean, and there on the sand, gasping for air, was a large pike.

"Oh Ivan-Tsarevich," it said, "save my life and throw me back into the

sea." Ivan-Tsarevich picked up the pike and threw it back into the sea and went on his way.

Finally the ball of yarn stopped right in front of a little hut which scuttled around on chicken legs.

"Little hut," cried Ivan-Tsarevich, "stand still please and let me in." The little hut stopped and Ivan-Tsarevich went inside. And there in the darkness was the old witch, Baba Yaga, snarling and baring her gruesome yellow teeth like a wild cat.

"What brings you here, young blood?" she hissed at him. Ivan-Tsarevich was too tired and hungry to be frightened by an old witch, so he just replied: "First give me a bath and something to eat, Baba Yaga, and then I'll tell you."

When she had done so, and he was well rested, he told her all about his adventures.

"I know all about Vassilissa the Wise," cackled Baba Yaga. "She is held prisoner by Koschtchev the Immortal, and unless you can find the way to his death, you will never defeat him, for he is strong and mighty beyond measure. But I will help you all I can and tell you that his death lies in the eye of a needle, that needle is in

an egg, the egg is in a duck and the duck is in a hare which he keeps locked up in a steel casket at the top of a huge oak tree."

The next morning, Ivan-Tsarevich set off to find Koschtchev the Immortal's death. Eventually he came to the great oak tree which seemed to go upwards for ever but at the top he saw, just as Baba Yaga had described, the steel casket, glinting in the sun. Poor Ivan-Tsarevich, the casket was too high for him to reach and he hung his head in despair. But, as everyone knows, a friend in need is a friend indeed and, quite out of the blue, a bear appeared and with his huge strength, uprooted the tree. As it toppled over, the casket crashed to the ground and shattered. Out from the broken casket darted a hare, but as it made ·off into the distance, another hare leapt on it and tore it apart. And just as Baba Yaga had predicted, a duck flew out of the hare's body carrying an egg in her beak and soared into the sky. Ivan-Tsarevich watched in astonishment as a drake flew out of nowhere and chased the duck across the skies until it was so frightened that it dropped the egg.

Ivan-Tsarevich ran hither and thither with his hands cupped

waiting to catch the precious egg, but to his horror it plummeted like a stone and landed in the middle of the deep sea with a huge splash. Ivan-Tsarevich wept bitterly. However was he to find a tiny egg in the sea! All was lost. And then, a miracle happened. All of a sudden, a pike came swimming towards him with the egg in its mouth. Ivan-Tsarevich reached out into the shallow water and took the egg, and the pike flicked its tail and disappeared. Quick as a flash Ivan-Tsarevich broke the egg open to find a needle inside. As he broke the eye off the needle, a shrill and piercing cry rent the air and in the nearby palace Koschtschev the Immortal died.

Ivan-Tsarevich ran like the wind to Koschtschev's palace where Vassilissa the Wise was waiting for him with outstretched arms. And so it was that they lived happily ever after and, to my knowledge, they were never parted again.

Anton Treetop

Once upon a time, two aged wise men were travelling through a cold and barren land. It was beginning to get dark and so, when they finally reached a small, cosy-looking farm-house, they decided to ask for a bed for the night. They were greeted by the farmer who told them that a rich fur merchant had taken the only guest room but that, if it was not too uncomfortable, they were welcome to the floor in the cattle stalls.

As midnight chimed, the wise men were awoken by strange, human cries for the farmer's wife was giving birth to her eighth child. One wise man turned to the other in alarm and said, "Go and help the poor woman, for she is in great pain."

His companion replied myster-iously, "I have already helped, more than they will ever know." The first wise man knew better than to ques-tion his friend and, anyway, the cries

suddenly stopped. In the farmhouse the farmer's wife was cradling her new-born son in her arms.

"What will become of this child?" asked the first wise man.

"Well," replied the other, "I predict that he will eventually become heir to the rich fur merchant who's asleep next door." Little did he know, but the merchant had also woken to the sounds of the baby being born and had gone outside for a breath of fresh air. When he had heard the wise man's prediction for the child's future, the rich merchant was absolutely furious, and spent the rest of the night thinking of ways to prevent the wise man's words from coming true.

By the next morning, he had invented a plan and so, at breakfast, he went to the farmer and said: "My good fellow, I am an extremely charitable man, and seeing that you already have far too many mouths to feed, why don't you and your wife let me take your new son and raise him as my own. My wife already has a baby daughter, and another one won't make any difference to her."

The farmer and his wife were kind people, but they were also very poor and, although they were heartbroken to part with their new baby, they both realised that he would stand the chance of a much better future with the rich fur merchant. And so, after a lot of thought and with heavy hearts, they agreed to the merchant's suggestion. The merchant then took the child and rode away quickly before they could change their minds. His journey took him through a great forest and when he came to the very thick of it, he wrapped up the child and tied it to the branches of a tall oak tree. Then, rubbing his hands together with glee, he rode off, congratulating himself that he had outwitted the wise man.

A little while later, a kindly old woodsman walked by the tree, and hearing the sounds of a baby's cry,

looked up and saw the tiny bundle hanging from the branches. He reached up, took the child gently into his arms, and returned home where he raised the baby and cared for him as if he was his own son. The woodsman's wife named the baby Anton, and because of the way the woodsman had found him, the villagers nicknamed him Anton Treetop. The tiny baby soon grew to be a fine young man, and his foster parents were extremely proud of him.

One day, however, and quite by chance, the wicked fur merchant happened to be travelling through the little village where Anton lived and he called in to the woodsman's

very house for a night's lodging. When he heard the woodsman calling his son Anton Treetop, he became curious and asked them how the boy had come by such a strange name. The woodsman was very obliging and proudly told the rich merchant of his part in rescuing Anton from the nearby forest.

Aha, thought the merchant, this is the same brat who caused me so much trouble all those years ago.

When he went to bed that night, the merchant spent another sleepless night, thinking of ways to get rid of Anton once and for all. In the morning, the treacherous merchant went to the woodsman and said: "I have important news for my family and I was wondering if you would allow your son Anton to deliver the message for me."

Anton was delighted to be of help, and immediately set off on the journey to the merchant's house. But in his hand, though he did not realise it, was a scroll which read:

"The bearer of this message should

be sold as a slave and taken away to a far and distant land."

After a full day's travelling, Anton was very tired and so he lay down on a soft bed of moss in a sun-drenched meadow and went to sleep. While he slept, two travellers came quietly past him and noticed the scroll which Anton was clutching. Being curious fellows, they gently took the paper out of Anton's hand. Fortunately for Anton, these were good and kind men, and when they realised that Anton was the victim of a cruel trick, they decided to turn the tables on the wicked merchant. So, they found another piece of paper and also wrote a message on it, but this time it read:

"The bearer of this message should be married to my daughter, for I have promised her to him. The wedding must take place before I return."

Then they pressed the new piece of paper into Anton's hand and went on their way, chuckling.

A little while later, Anton woke up and hurried on to the merchant's house. When he arrived and had delivered the message, the merchant's wife was rather surprised by her husband's strange command. But, because he was a brutal man, she dared not disobey him and so the bewildered Anton, and the even

more surprised merchant's daughter, were married that very day.

The next few weeks were the happiest Anton had ever known, and he and his new wife were soon the best of friends and very much in love. But good things must come to an end, and the merchant returned home. When he saw Anton, hatred flashed in his eyes and his mouth fell open, but he was a crafty man, and instead of throwing himself into a rage and revealing his true nature, he began to think of another plot. When his wife explained to him what had happened, and he realised that his trick had been turned against him, the merchant went up to Anton and said: "Now that you are my son-in-law, you must prove to me that you deserve the love of my daughter and the enormous wealth that you will inherit when I die. So, young Anton Treetop, you must go the Northern Lands and ask Queen Louhi, who rules that land, what it is which brings a man the greatest happiness of all. Go now, boy, and do not return until you are sure you have my answer."

Poor Anton set off, not realising that no one had ever returned alive from the Northern Lands.

He rode across hills and forests, swam rivers and lakes, until he came to a vast cliff which loomed above him, on top of which stood a giant. Anton was terrified, and felt that his young life might end there and then, so he was surprised when the giant asked, in a friendly manner: "Where are you off to, my lad?"

"I'm going to the Northern Lands, sir," replied Anton, "to ask Queen Louhi what it is which brings a man the greatest happiness."

"In that case," said the giant, "perhaps you would also ask her what is causing all the fruit in my beautiful garden to rot."

"I'll certainly ask her for you, sir," said Anton, and he went on his way. He had not got much further when his ears rang with the sound of a loud booming — an earth-shattering sound. Anton looked up and saw another giant hammering mightily on the door of an enormous castle. The giant heard Anton's quaking footsteps and turned to look at him. His angry expression faded suddenly and a rather foolish grin spread across his moon-like face. "Where are you going, young man?" he asked.

Again Anton replied that he was going to see Queen Louhi to ask her what it is which brings a man the greatest happiness. The giant scratched his huge head thoughtfully and asked rather shyly: "Would you also ask her where on earth I've put the key to my front door? If you do, I'll give you all my treasure."

Anton said he would, and went on his way again until he came across a third giant who was perched in the

uppermost branches of a large tree. In his hand he held a roasting spit on which an elk was roasting over a fire on the ground. When the giant saw Anton, he called to him: "Come over here, my lad, and I'll give you something to eat, for you look in need of it."

As it happened, Anton was very hungry, and so he raced over to the tree, where he and the giant feasted together. While they ate, Anton told him about his journey.

"Well," said the giant, when he had finished, "if you are going there, do you think you would ask Queen Louhi how I could get out of this wretched tree?"

"Of course I will," said Anton, and thanking the giant for his meal, he went on his way.

Just before he reached Louhi's kingdom, he came to a wide river, where an old woman was stooped in a rowing boat, moored by the bank.

"Will you take a weary traveller across the river?" asked Anton.

"Of course I will," the old crone replied, "that's my job, more's the pity." So Anton clambered in to the boat and the old woman started to row him across the river.

Just before they reached the other side, the old woman looked up at him

curiously and asked, just as the giants had done, where he was going. When Anton explained, she asked: "When you get to good Queen Louhi, would you remember a poor old woman to her and ask her how I can leave this awful job of mine. After forty years of ferrying travellers across the same old river, it does get very dull." Anton gave her his word that he would ask, and when they reached the bank, he thanked her and went on his way.

Very soon he saw a signpost which directed him to Queen Louhi's house. When he arrived, he found the door was on the latch, so he let himself in. Queen Louhi was not at home that day, but Anton found her

daughter kneading dough in the kitchen. Anton introduced himself and the girl asked him to sit down.

"My mother is away at the moment," she said, "but if it's important, you're welcome to wait here until she gets back." But, when Anton told the girl the reason for his visit, she dropped her dough on the floor in amazement. "My goodness, it's just as well for you that my mother isn't here, she'd have you beheaded for wasting her time with such silly questions. Besides, you're mortal. She cannot abide mortals."

Anton just sat there, feeling rather stupid and very scared. However, the girl took pity on him, partly because

she had seen the disappointment in his face, and partly because he was very handsome. So she said gently: "Don't worry, I think I can help you. When my mother comes home tonight, you can hide behind that stove over there and listen while I ask your questions for you, but when you have heard the answers you must leave as quietly as you can or she'll have you for supper."

So that night, as Queen Louhi's footsteps sounded in the hall outside, Anton crept behind the stove and waited. Queen Louhi greeted her daughter warmly and then asked if there had been any visitors that day.

"No one in particular," the girl replied casually, "except there was a young man who called, wanting to know the answers to this and that, but when I told him you weren't here he went off to ask someone else."

"Who else in the world knows as much as I do?" snapped Louhi. "Did he tell you what he wanted?"

"As a matter of fact he did," replied the girl. "Firstly he wanted to know what it is which brings a man the greatest happiness."

"Huh," scoffed Louhi, "I'm the only person who knows the answer to that. To achieve the greatest happiness, a man should till the soil and grow corn. What else did he want to know?"

"Then he wanted to know what was causing a giant's fruit to rot in his garden."

"That's easy," boasted Louhi, "there must be a worm in the garden. If the giant crushes the worm, all his fruit will flourish again. What else?"

"Well, he wanted to know where another giant had left his door key."

"It is under the front door step; if he lifts up the stone he will find it."

"Then he wanted to know how a giant, who has spent all his life crouched in a tree, could get down to the ground."

"That's easier still," said Louhi, who was beginning to enjoy herself.

"He must touch the trunk of the tree with an alder branch. Then all the branches will turn to gold and snap off and the giant will fall to the ground with them."

"There was just one more question," said the girl. "How can the old woman who ferries people across the river give up her job?"

"Easy!" said Louhi. "The next time a traveller wants to cross, she should take him to the other side of the river and leap out first, then she should push the boat in to the river again with her foot and say, 'I'm off now, you'll have to be the ferryman.' My goodness, what a tiresome young man he must be."

Anton decided that it was time he left, so he crept out and ran like the wind to the old ferry woman, who was waiting for him. Very wisely,

Anton waited until he was standing safely on the bank across the river before he gave her the answer to her question. When he repeated Louhi's instructions, the old woman's face lit up and she thanked him gratefully and sat rubbing her hands in glee, waiting for the next passenger.

Anton made great haste and soon he came to the huge giant in the tree.

"Have you got my answer?" shouted the giant. Anton replied that he had, and quickly grabbed an alder branch. At the first touch, the branches of the tree turned to gold and fell to the ground, bringing the delighted giant with them. Although the giant was very insistent, Anton refused to take any more payment for his kindness than a few golden twigs which he said would make good riding crops.

Next, Anton came to the giant who was still hammering furiously on his front door.

"Try looking under your front door step," suggested Anton. The giant did so and, just as Louhi said, there was his key. The giant was overjoyed and so grateful that he showered Anton with wondrous treasures.

Anton struggled on under the weight of his treasure until, finally, he came to the last giant.

"There's a worm in your garden, giant," Anton shouted up to him. "If you kill the worm then your fruit will stop rotting." This giant was even more delighted than the others had been, and he gave Anton his very finest horse to ride home on.

And so, at long last, Anton finally arrived back at the merchant's house.

"Well," snapped the merchant, who was very angry to see that Anton had survived the journey, "did you get the answer to my question?"

"Yes I did," said Anton. "Queen Louhi says that man achieves greatest happiness by tilling the soil and growing corn." The merchant was furious. Not only had Anton come home with untold riches, but he had also gained the answer to his question. And since the merchant was a greedy man, he decided to go to the Northern Lands himself to see if he could do better than Anton Treetop. He also thought he might ask Queen Louhi how on earth he could get rid of the young man for ever.

That very day, the merchant saddled his horse and headed north. After many days, he reached the great river, where an old woman sat huddled in a tiny rowing boat.

"Take me across, my good woman," commanded the merchant.

"Certainly, sir," she replied, "it will give me great pleasure."

But, just as they reached the far side of the river, the old woman leapt out of the boat and pushed it back across the water, and as it disappeared into the distance, she shouted after it: "I'm off, I've done my forty years, now it's your turn."

So the grand fur merchant became a ferryman, and, just as the wise man had predicted, Anton Treetop lived a charmed and happy life and inherited all the merchant's wealth.

The Castle East of the Sun and West of the Moon

Once upon a time there was a miller, an extremely handsome young man and a perfect son, who worked with such vigour and good will that his parents, who were getting old, were spared all the back-breaking tasks of the mill.

The young man took a great deal of pride in his work and was understandably very angry when he noticed that a mysterious thief was raiding his corn store every night. When he saw that his parents were becoming anxious too, his temper suddenly snapped.

"This must stop at once," the young miller said to himself and he decided that every night, just before it got dark, he would climb into the barn loft and hide behind a sack of corn to lie in wait for the villain.

This he did, and for several long and dreary nights he lay in wait for the culprit but the thief stopped coming. And then, one night, just as the miller was about to give up and return to the mill house, three beautiful white doves fluttered gracefully in through a tiny window at the top of the barn and started pecking the sacks of corn furiously, right before the astonished young man's eyes. The miller had never seen birds with such an appetite and realised that they must have flown a long way to be so hungry.

When the doves had eaten their fill, a strange thing happened. They suddenly shed their snow-white feathers like cloaks, and were transformed into three beautiful girls, more beautiful than the miller had ever seen before.

The young man was agog with astonishment but the girls just sat

down together on the corn sacks and chatted away merrily as if this was an everyday event. They were so absorbed in conversation that they did not even notice when the miller, who was terribly curious, crept out of his hiding place and stole one of the feather cloaks. Indeed, it was only when the girls got up to leave that they noticed one was missing and although they searched frantically, they did not find the cloak or the miller. At last, as the slight hints of morning streaked the sky, two of the girls picked up their cloaks, draped them hurriedly over their shoulders, turned back into doves and flew away.

The remaining dove maiden just sat down on the empty corn sacks and wept bitterly. At the sight of her tears the miller's heart melted, and because he could never bear to see anyone cry, least of all a pretty girl, he came out of hiding and spoke to her.

"Please don't cry. Stay here with me and be my wife."

"It's all right for you," said the dove maiden, who seemed not the least surprised by the sudden appearance of the miller or his proposal, "but if I don't find my cloak and fly home before sunrise I will die and it's almost too late now." At this, her face

puckered once more and she buried her head in her handkerchief.

"I'll give you back your cloak," said the miller, "but only if you promise

on your word of honour that you will marry me."

"Even if I promised," she replied, "you would have to leave your mill and come and live with me in my castle, which lies east of the sun and west of the moon in the enchanted forest. You see, I am really a princess but there is a spell on my sisters and me which keeps us prisoners by day and doves by night. It's really a miserable life; I'm sure you wouldn't be very happy."

"I still want to marry you," said the miller, and he handed her back the feather cloak to seal their bargain. Just before she put it on, she turned to him and said: "If your love is strong enough, it could break the spell, but you'll never find the way to the castle east of the sun and west of the moon, so you may as well forget you ever saw me."

By now, the young miller was deeply in love and he knew then and there that he would never be able to forget her. So, that very night, he set off in search of the castle. He ran and ran, up hills and down dales, through forests and across rivers and whenever he saw anyone he would stop and ask them the way to the castle but, alas, no one had ever heard of it.

After many weeks, the miller

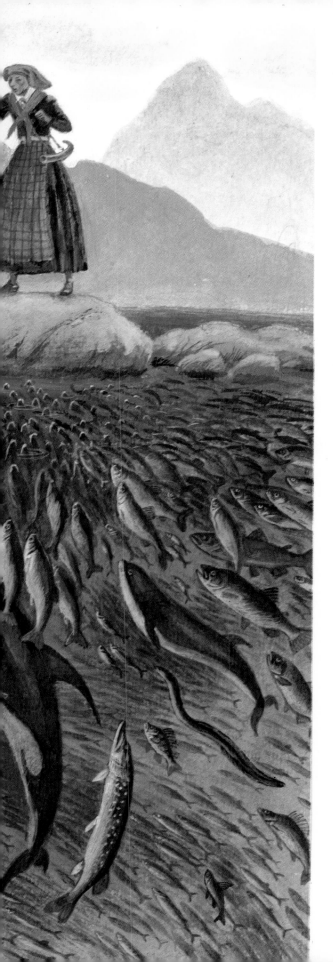

chanced on a small cottage by the sea. When he knocked on the door an elderly woman, with a face like a rosy crab-apple, greeted him and invited him inside, for it was a very cold night and the young man looked exhausted. After a time, when the miller had rested a little, he asked her if she had ever heard of the castle east of the sun and west of the moon and she replied: "Not personally, my dear, but I am the ruler of all the sea creatures and perhaps one of my subjects will know. Tomorrow morning I shall take you to meet them, but now it's late and, as you see, I need my beauty sleep." With that, she shuffled off to bed, chuckling merrily.

Early next morning, the miller and the elderly wise woman, for that was what she was, went down to the sea shore and, standing on a rock facing the waves, the wise woman blew with all her might into an ancient hunting horn. The eerie sound disturbed the calm surface of the water, which began to blister with the heads of thousands of strange sea creatures who peered curiously at the miller. When she asked them if they knew of the castle, they all shook their heads in unison and disappeared.

The elderly wise woman turned to the crest-fallen miller and said: "How

disappointing for you, my dear, but don't give up yet. Why not go on a little farther and see my mother who is the ruler of all the land animals — she may be able to help." The miller said goodbye to the old lady, and thanked her for all her help.

"Don't mention it, my dear," she replied. "Just follow your nose until you reach the golden forest."

So the miller set off again and, as the sun began to set, he arrived at his destination. This time he was greeted by an even older lady who promised to consult the land animals about the castle the next day.

After a good night's sleep, the miller found himself standing in the bright morning sunlight in a large clearing in the middle of a forest, which gleamed and shimmered with a mysterious golden light. Suddenly, the eerie sound of the second old lady's horn rang in his ears. The land animals were as swift to answer their summons as the sea creatures had been. They were all very apologetic, but they had never heard of the castle east of the sun and west of the moon either.

"Don't despair, young man," said the wise woman. "You have one more chance. Why not go and see my mother, who is the ruler of all the

birds in the sky." The miller thanked her kindly and said that he would do that. But he thought to himself, this lady is older than anyone I have ever seen before, and I dread to think how ancient her mother must be! She was, indeed, very, very ancient, as the miller discovered when he arrived at her cottage, which was perched like a

pimple on top of the highest mountain in the land. Her craggy but kindly old face seemed older even than the mountain winds which had weathered it, but her spirit was bright and cheerful and she too promised to help the young man.

So, the next day, the miller found himself standing beside the ancient wise woman on the mountain's edge. She coughed and spluttered into her hunting horn and, sure enough, thousands of birds came soaring towards them, only to soar away again when not one of them proved able to help the miller.

When the last, tiniest sparrow had shaken its head mournfully, the miller's plucky heart sank into his boots.

"Wait a minute," croaked the ancient wise woman, "the eagle has not arrived yet."

At that very moment a black speck appeared on the horizon, becoming gradually larger as it swooped towards them, and soon the miller was able to make out the shape of the biggest eagle he had ever seen. It landed rather clumsily, and was obviously exhausted.

"I am late, I know," it said, "but I have flown all day. I have come from the castle east of the sun and west of

the strangest, thought the miller, and he shivered as the bitter mountain winds whipped round him, freezing his hands and face to blocks of ice.

They arrived at dusk and the castle looked very forbidding in the half-light. The miller's first impression was a gloomy one. Indeed, it looked to

the moon, many miles away."

These long awaited words were music to the miller's ears and he was so overcome with emotion that he leapt forward and kissed the eagle's beak. The next thing he knew, he was clinging to the eagle's neck and they were winging their way to the castle east of the sun and west of the moon at last! Of all the strange things that have happened to me recently, flying on the back of an eagle must surely be

him much more like a grim fortress than a princess's palace and he wondered to himself if he could be happy in such a cold-looking place. Then he remembered his beloved princess and without further ado, he screwed up his courage and strode inside.

He found the dove maidens playing a rather miserable game of patience in the monstrous entrance hall. His princess rushed up to him

and, smothering him with hugs and kisses, said impatiently: "What took you so long, I have been waiting an age for you. But now you're here the proven strength of your love has almost broken the spell. You only have one more task to perform. You must come with me at once and cut down the evil rose bush which rules the dark forest and holds the power source of the spell."

Armed with a sharp axe, the princess led the miller into the heart of the forest, where a beautiful rose tree stood. The miller was a wise young man and knew that appearances could be deceptive, so he felt no pity as he felled the rose tree with one almighty blow of the axe. As it hit the ground, there was a deafening crack of thunder and a bolt of lightning struck the ground in front of them. The couple cowered together in terror, and shut their eyes tight. When, finally, they had enough courage to open them, they looked around and saw that a miracle had happened. The mysterious forest had disappeared. In its place were fields and meadows carpeted in primroses and swathed in bright sunlight. In the distance they could see the castle, no longer grey and forbidding but now the colour of burnished gold and

worthy of any fairy-tale princess there has ever been. The spell was broken at last!

All the princesses were terribly grateful to the miller, and none more so than his bride-to-be who began to plan their wedding. Now that his adventures were over at last, the miller began to think about his parents, whom he had almost forgotten in all the excitement. How worried they must be, he thought, and decided he would go and speak to the princess.

"Of course you must go to them," said the princess. "I will lend you my fastest horse so that you won't have to be away long, but you must not get off him on any account, or the spell's power will start to work again and we will be parted for ever."

The miller set off immediately and because the horse ran as fast as the wind he arrived at his parents' mill the very same day. The old couple were overjoyed to see their son again, and listened intently to the stories of his adventures. And although his mother begged him to come inside and warm himself by the fire, the princess's voice rang loud and clear in the miller's ears and he refused to dismount.

Then an awful thing happened.

Just as the miller was about to leave, a squawking chicken flew up into the air in front of him and startled the horse which reared up, threw the miller to the ground and bolted into the distance.

Weeks passed and the miller, who was more miserable than anyone in the history of fairy tales, gave up hope of ever seeing his beloved princess

again and prepared himself to die of a broken heart.

But then, one morning, an elegant carriage drew up outside the mill and the princess stepped out. When the two had embraced for the hundredth time, the princess explained: "When your horse returned to the castle, I saw that the girth was broken and I realised that you had had an accident

and hadn't deliberately disobeyed me. That is why I was able to come and find you."

So the miller and his princess took his mother and father back with them to the castle east of the sun and west of the moon and they all lived in a state of blissful happiness ever after.